COMMUNICATING IN THE WORKPLACE